# Opus

Also by Pip Griffin

Published by Ginninderra Press
*The Climb Back*

Published by Pohutukawa Press
*Salt Lake* (2004)
*Last song: the first year* (2007)
*Ani Lin: the journey of a Chinese Buddhist nun* (2010)
*Margaret Caro: the extraordinary life of a pioneering dentist,
New Zealand 1848–1938: her story in verse* (2021)
(Highly Commended, Society of Women Writers NSW
Book Awards 2020 – Poetry)
*Envoi: Ted Rutter's selected poems 1990–2017* (2021, editor)
*Virginia and Katherine: The Secret Diaries* (2021)
(Winner, Society of Women Writers NSW
Book Awards 2022 – Poetry)

By Pip Griffin with Colleen Keating
*Mood Indigo* (Picaro Poets, 2020)

Pip Griffin

# Opus
## A Life With Music

## Acknowledgements

Some poems in this collection previously appeared in *Last song: the first year*, *The Climb Back*, *Mood Indigo*, *Poetry Matters*, *Women's Ink*, *The Mozzie*, *tamba*, and the anthologies *Class Act* and *Women's Work*.

My very special thanks to Norm Neill and the members of the Wednesday Night Poets group at Writing NSW, Geoff Lucas and Harbourside Poets, Sydney City Fellowship of Australian Writers group and Mark Mahemoff for critique and encouragement; Colleen Keating for affirmation, invaluable critique, editing, shaping and proofreading; Jenny Stewart for her friendship and support; John Griffin for his evocative cover design and the editors of Ginninderra Press for their ongoing encouragement and dedication to publishing poetry.

*Opus – A Life With Music*
ISBN 978 1 76109 570 2
Copyright © text Pip Griffin 2023
Cover: John Griffin

First published 2023 by
**GINNINDERRA PRESS**
PO Box 3461 Port Adelaide 5015
www.ginninderrapress.com.au

# Contents

A song to remember
- Mayday — 11
- Party piece — 13
- Church choir — 14
- The cello — 15
- Young person's guide — 16
- A song to remember — 17
- Rachmaninov's Second Piano Concerto — 18
- The Student Prince — 19
- First dance — 20
- Concerto for two violins — 21

Air on a G String
- My mother's song — 25
- Little cakes of soap — 27
- Keeper — 28
- Sisters — 30
- Chasing his dreams — 32
- Bach's Air on a G String — 34

New song
- Rock 'n' roll — 37
- Awakes my heart — 38
- First Brahms then poetry — 39
- New song — 40
- When the dancing stopped — 41
- The Dream of Gerontius — 42

Duet
- The Dave Brubeck Quartet — 45
- Concerto for girl and harpsichords — 46
- Free love — 47

| | |
|---|---:|
| Duet | 48 |
| Ukulele boys | 49 |

## Right of passage
| | |
|---|---:|
| Sibelius 2 | 53 |
| Sibelius 2 reprised | 55 |
| Vaughan Williams' 5th Symphony | 56 |
| Some moments | 57 |
| Right of passage | 58 |
| Jerusalem | 59 |
| Calcutta | 61 |
| Journey from the centre of the earth | 62 |
| That houri's dance | 63 |
| The hardest word | 64 |
| Resurrection | 65 |
| Listening to Tchaikovsky | 66 |

## Cameo
| | |
|---|---:|
| Cameo at Hanging Rock | |
| Womadelaide 2001 | 70 |
| Libertango | 71 |
| Philip Glass in Florence | 72 |
| Mahler 1 | 74 |

## Pavane
| | |
|---|---:|
| Pavane | 77 |
| Leonard Cohen was a brave man | 78 |
| Water music | 79 |
| Every time we say goodbye… | 80 |
| Loch Lomond | 81 |
| Jupiter again | 82 |
| Leura Gardens | 83 |
| Little Golden Bay | 84 |

| | |
|---|---:|
| Notes | 85 |

> Music is a shortcut to memory
> – Cassie Tongue

Some of my earliest memories are of sitting at my mother's piano (sadly, I never heard her play) pounding the keys, and of later begging her to let me have lessons. Later still, she projected her frustrated ambitions on to me, deciding I would be a concert pianist!

This collection begins with a poem I wrote a few years ago after hearing Chopin's Waltz in E Major on ABC Classic FM. I was swept back to when I was thirteen years old.

My gentle piano teacher encouraged me to learn the waltz by heart as a 'party piece' to reduce the anxiety I felt when asked to play for an audience. Writing 'Party piece' released a flow of memories defined by music and a steady flow of new poems.

I am grateful to Norm Neill, convenor of the Wednesday Night Poets group at Writing NSW, for suggesting these poems would be suitable for an autobiographical series. Writing them has brought home to me the profound place music has had in my life. It has brought, and continues to bring me, great joy.

# A song to remember

Music…that which comes closest to expressing the inexpressible
– Aldous Huxley

# Mayday

In your small solemn face I see myself at five or six
hair neatly braided
indomitable, self-contained
my child's world all those years ago
beyond your comprehension
small town time warp
a doll, some storybooks, schooldays
the beach, my uncle's farm
BBC wireless call sign with breakfast
anxiety an undercurrent to my cosseted existence
yet the war seemed far from us
Mum's roasts and sago pudding
Dad exempt due to his game leg
I too young to comprehend my brother's absence
or the words *deprivation   valour   Guadalcanal.*

His safe return brought smiling relatives
loud laughter and the clink of glasses keeping me awake.
I do remember VJ Day –
the streamers, whistles, wooden rattles
people drinking, dancing in the streets.

My brother (that gaunt stranger)
was quick to marry the girl who'd waited
their wedding unforgettable
because I crossed the road to feed the ducks
and was knocked down by a bicycle –
the blood, the fuss, the searching for a doctor
scarring my memory as deeply as the sharp slap on the legs
I (child whom parents never had to punish) suffered
with silent, searing indignation on my first day of school.

You, little girl, safe with your mother, sister
you'll grow up to a world beyond my comprehension –
perhaps even beyond your own.

# Party piece

She hears the lilting Chopin waltz
suggested by her teacher
for 'party piece' occasions
to show off to her mother's friends.

The mother,
task-mistress of her daughter's piano practice,
dreamed a brilliant musical career
denied her when she was young.

At thirteen,
after her father's near-death
failed piano exam
new house, new school
she became an anxious teenager
who donned a Kevlar coat
to shield her real self from the world.

At sixteen,
the Chopin piece she learned to love
accompanied her coming out.
Performance fear receded.
She cast off the coat –
new confidence propelled her into womanhood.

At eighteen,
leaving her hometown, she promised
to take her last exam.
Instead, the newborn self took charge.
Piano was abandoned for her larger life
but music was always with her –
a velvet garment of first love.

# Church choir

In Geography class
she sits behind a girl
whose short, brown, wavy hair
she gazes at, wishing it were hers.
As friendship flourishes
the girl tells her she is a chorister
at Holy Trinity.

Though her parents shun the church
they encourage her to join
knowing their solitary daughter
craves company.

Shadowing her new friend
to church hall practice
she joins a motley group.
She finds her voice.

The red cassock's weight
the rituals
the weekly tedium of sermons
are difficult to bear
but at Christmas
being at one with harmonies
and plainsong soaring to the vault
fills her with transcendent joy
and turns her to belief.

# The cello

Playing lifts you out of yourself into a delirious place
– Jacqueline du Pré

She is a still quite-timid teen
when the cello finds her.

She joins the orchestra
eager to play a violin
but the music teacher
tells her she has 'cello hands'.

He is right.
She falls in love with the sturdy body
she can wrap her legs around
its response to fingering
the resonance
of bow on strings.

In collegiate music making
more satisfying than church choirs
she feels complete.

The music learnt then
never leaves her.

## Young person's guide

In the hot pool, four of them relax
after first day of music camp,

straight into playing Britten's
*Young Person's Guide to the Orchestra.*

Sulphurous fumes swirl round them.
Her eyes weep – last thing she wants with him so close.

He turns to face her: 'How did you go today?'
She knows her face is red

her body bulgy
in her swimming togs;

her shy heart staggers
as she struggles to untie her tongue.

'It was the best day of my life!'
He smiles then turns toward

the slim red-headed flautist on his right
whose green eyes gaze at him adoringly.

# A song to remember

In the Odeon
three school friends
giggle
loll in velvet-upholstered seats
in charged half-light.

Cadbury's Caramello clutched
to burgeoning chests
their romance with celluloid begins.

They're wild about Cornel
their handsome heart throb
playing Chopin –
heroic Pole
passionate composer
and lover of cross-dressed George Sand.

His hands pound the crashing chords
of the Polonaise
into their eager bodies.
Blood spatters
the keyboard.

# Rachmaninov's Second Piano Concerto

In the audience
at their first ever adult concert
two cello students vibrate
to tuning up discordant as a penguin rookery.

They're seated on the cellists' side
a front row view
and eye the dreamy Italian leader,
precious instrument between his thighs.

Conductor and soloist walk onstage
to restrained applause;
the soloist adjusts the piano stool;
the cellist's spider fingers grip his bow;
the baton poises
then swoops
in silence as profound as death.

The opening sostenuto piano chords –
dah   dah
dah   dah
dah   dah
dah
dah dah dah
dah!
thrust Slavic passion
into their receptive souls.

## The Student Prince

In ugly duckling time
of pimply faces and chubby thighs
of adolescence straining to emerge
from bodies trapped in drab serge tunics
two friends hear about a musical
in brand-new Cinemascope –
beg their parents to let them go.

The prince's songs are lip-synched –
suave Hollywood actor
honey-voiced Italian-American tenor.

The girls want to be German
want to be bold, *stein*-flourishing students
want to be the pretty waitress
want to be the princess bride.

On the way home, arms linked
they march in many-coloured caps
to *Gaudeamus Igitur*
quiver with the prince's touch
burn with the rejected waitress
sing
*Drink, Drink, Drink!*
*Deep in my Heart, Dear*
and *Beloved*
throats strained
spirits waltzing.

# First dance

Reader, I married him – *Jane Eyre*

You wear your new blue taffeta dress
heart palpitating under the ruched bodice
palms clammy

side-eying the blasé boys across the hall
your body goose-bumping
waiting to be asked to dance.

'Moon River' plays on the sound system
sweet music that sways you towards love.
One of the boys is a year above you

tall   rugby player   smooth talker
you'll die for him if he asks
but if he does what can you say to him

you shy bumble-tongued teen
fed romance by the classics?
He might be your Mr Rochester

Heathcliff   Mr Darcy
but will he ask you to dance?

# Concerto for two violins

The past is a foreign country – L.P. Hartley

you read *The Go-Between*
and buy a record
of the music it invokes
and while you listen
see yourself
and an other

lithe
graceful
two Gibran spirit forms
souls congruent
in perfect harmony
in dialogue miraculous

andante
adagio
taut with longing
liquid with light

now together
now apart
soaring
spiralling
embracing

forever

# Air on a G String

> Music is life itself
> – Louis Armstrong

# My mother's song

Returning to New Zealand
shipboard with parents, brothers, sisters
from Tahiti where they'd lived a year in 1910
while Grandfather built houses for white people
they sang around the piano nightly.

The Herr Doktor revealed he was a singing teacher
said she should be trained to sing in opera
he would take her with him to Vienna –
such talent could not be denied.
The cost? All would be taken care of.

Grandfather, of course, said no.
She was too young, too gentle, too naïve
too shy, too nervous.
He had other plans for her: a suitable job, a safe marriage.
There was no more to be said.

I have one photo of her wedding day
thin then, pretty, with a veil and train
my father and the family proud beside her.

I never knew her parents, dead when I was born.
What happened to her brothers, those fine boys?
Her sisters lived nearby, visited when I was growing up
as did my father's brothers and their wives.
Jim was the only one she ever mentioned –
killed in Italy, 1916.

The mother I knew cared for her children
then her ailing husband.
Loyal.
Past buried.
Life half-lived.

I never heard my mother sing.

# Little cakes of soap

Rejected as a soldier
you were still away too often
bringing back those little cakes of soap
to add to my collection.

One summer near war's end
you bought a section near the beach.
From under hedgerows' leaf-littered cool
I watched you build a wooden shed
and plant swedes and potatoes
in the East Coast heat.

Horseflies with bulging iridescent eyes
sucked my pony's blood
as you, lead rein held firm, limped
along the narrow, shivery-grassed tracks.
I can't remember if we talked.
I was afraid of you – the man some kids
teased could be my grandfather.

Did your relentless digging in that searing sun
bring on the stroke then two more seizures?
The year that I turned ten
there were too many visits to the hospital
where the wards tasted of fear –
and you a damaged stranger in our house
confined in co-dependence with my mother
until your death.

# Keeper

Home after school
attune to subtle signs
I know she's been doing it again.

Her eyes are somewhere else
as I talk about my day –
my A-plus English essay mark

the brash girls who shun me
snigger in class
and make Miss Williams cry.

She says she's been spring cleaning
is exhausted
feels a migraine coming on.

When she's gone upstairs to rest
I go into the pantry
and reach behind the peach preserves.

I know she shoves the bottle
right to the back.
The level's down again.

Face flaming, I take it to the sink
pour half away
and fill it up with water.

At thirteen I've become her keeper –
my best friend whom I adore
who chivvies me to practise scales

who's always made me share
the burden of her negative emotions
and bitter disappointments

whose own ambitions dribbled away
like the gin I watch
drain slowly down the kitchen sink.

## Sisters

In Camperdown Rest Park a small girl
        reaches for her sister's hand.

The younger one's half the other's height
        as, hand in hand, they walk away from me.

I have a photo of my sister, one hand
        in mine, a cigarette in the other

she smiling, good looking
        perhaps twenty, me five or six.

We're at the agricultural show
        and look happy to be together.

Who took the snap I've no idea
        but peering into shadows

I see an absent sister –
        away at training college

away beach camping with her friends
        then away teaching school.

I feel my swell of awe and pride
        to see her singing with a dance band

her total confidence in acting
        in amateur theatricals.

Then she was away with a much older man
        who took her to Australia.

We swapped letters and photos for a while –
>    she looked happy cuddling her children.

I feel the ache of missing her.
>    How often did she hold my hand?

## Chasing his dreams

In a picture at an exhibition
I saw an eager face
not unlike my own

could have been my sister's
among the group of twenty-somethings
snapped at a motor show in 1948
free spirits
dressed to kill

she left home for Australia
when I was five
sent back photos of her babies
one each year
easy as breath

she'd been head girl at high school
champion swimmer
an actor
dance band singer
ardent teacher
a person I should emulate
until she ran off with a man
our mother disproved of

I saw my sister three times only
in adulthood
the last not long before her death

she reminisced about her husband
beloved tyrant
achingly missed
they had twelve children
while they moved around the country
chasing his dreams

her face still eager
luminous
as she talked of him.

# Bach's Air on a G String

Arriving at my sister's funeral
        (a virtual stranger
only recently re-met)

I was greeted by the Air
        that filled the chapel
together with her grieving children.

Though her funeral service is a blur
        the music lives forever in my body
soundtrack to her sudden violent death.

I knew her only briefly
        and had few memories –
was left with guilt and deep regret

a new family who showed me love
        and a plangent refrain
that keens my loss each time I hear it.

# New song

Music promises to deliver us to our inner lives
– Anna Goldsworthy

# Rock 'n' roll

First year training college
the women's hostel commonroom
lounge chairs   Coca Cola   a record player

five students gyrate to Bill Haley's
American dance craze –
nineteen fifties' college revolution

hair flying, their supple bodies practise moves
tense with longing for romance
aglow with youth and laughter

they want to defy the curfew
dance all night   drink alcohol
swagger with US sailors down midnight streets

pash in the dark alley behind the hostel
swoon to the pressure of eager lips
firmly rebuff wandering hands

sneak through their bedroom windows
hearts in mouths
drink hot cocoa and giggle until 5 a.m.

they want to shock their parents
they want to have secrets
they want life to begin.

## Awakes my heart

In pod of privacy
buoyed by cover of the water's thwack
you sing the poignant aria

its alto range effortless for your voice.
You've never sung at home
that hushed invalid's domain

where none will raise their voice
but in this new home of share rooms
communal meals   loud young women

you find yours: learning to shout
when finished with the bathroom
or communal iron

or when somebody's boyfriend is on the phone
chatting with new found girlfriends
going to jazz clubs   coffee bars   movies

discovering cigarettes   Pimms No 1
and boyfriends.
You join the drama club

write satiric verses for the revue
revelling in the laughter
the songs receive.

As you bow with fellow players
the clapping and the cheering
emboldens your awakened self.

# First Brahms then poetry

A frosty, chilblained morning –
music surges
from the draughty post-war lecture room.
She shivers to be let in;
portentous chaconnes
and tumultuous themes
sweep from jeopardy
to promise and exhilaration;
seize
excite
envelop her
carry her into the unknown.

The English lecturer
plays Brahms each week,
a prelude to their study
of the poets
Brasch, Baxter, Beaglehole
Curnow and Campbell
Fairburn, Johnson
Mason and Voght.

Emotions bared
poetry takes hold
and dances with her.

# New song

Choruses surround her –
more complex than church hymns
more worldly than school choir
more testing than playing piano.

In tarantella student halls
with cacophony of strangers
quiet voices are not heard.
She learns to shout.

Bill Haley, Elvis, shake her
wake her
to dance with actors
artists and musicians

who introduce her to cool jazz
in coffee bars in Cuba Street
and joy of unimagined liaisons
that take her to the edge.

Hearing James K. Baxter
recite his works one night
she is propelled to poetry
she hopes will save her soul.

# When the dancing stopped

Who is she now

that men who've wooed her
artists, actors, passionate all
have left now playing has lost its thrall

Who is she now

those men chase after worldly prey
the haughty girls who make them weep
as she wept when the dancing stopped

Who is she now

left stricken, naked on the stage
soul aching, duped by artifice
a graceless, laughable naif.

Who is she now?

# The Dream of Gerontius

Salvaging jaggalled shards of self
she joins 'music appreciation,'
a lunchtime retreat for bookish types
wanting to avoid cafeteria brouhaha –
in her case, the artist, her bête noir,
who's flinging up an abstract mural.

The music lecturer
is not unlike her high school teacher –
short, intense, obsessed with Elgar
who plays 'Enigma Variations',
'Pomp and Circumstance' and the du Pré concerto.
He encourages her to join his choir.

During weeks of preparation
she finds new voice.
At the concert, she is at one with angels.
Hope hurtles her forward.

# Duet

Music is the language of the emotions
– Anne Boyd

# The Dave Brubeck Quartet

At twenty she shares a flat with friends
>	in half a house that clambers up the hill in Thorndon

adds a Brubeck record to her Bach and Brahms
>	buys a ticket to his Town Hall concert

and sits alone amongst expectant fans
>	taut as drum skins begging to be played.

Brain on fire with crooked rhythms
>	her body jitterbugs to teasing riffs

the dry martini saxophone stirs her spine
>	dizzying drumming pummels her solar plexus

and there is Brubeck – bespectacled face beaming
>	striding syncopated chords across the keyboard.

# Concerto for girl and harpsichords

She's with choir friends
a museum gallery   a Sunday afternoon

two harpsichords with Baroque bird motifs
yellowed keys expectant
face an audience perched
between rows of stuffed birds
and jars of twisted creatures fixed in formalin

had they gone to hear the Bach recital
or did they stumble upon it –
music-hungry students
searching for distraction
on a dull Wellington weekend?

contrapuntal silver bouncing
from keyboard to keyboard
from violin   to viola   to cello
the harpsichords' duelling staccato
dances deep into her.

# Free love

Working and fancy free
we all had boyfriends
who took us to parties
jazz bars
a movie now and then.
They visited the Thorndon house
but never stayed for dinner.

When our landlady was away
her granddaughter moved into her apartment
with her lover.
We'd hear them through the wall.
Sometimes she swanned downstairs
wearing a negligee
and a smug smile for us
whose fear of getting pregnant kept us chaste.

We all had hometown stories
of fallen girls – town bikes –
both pitied and despised
yet this girl our age who had some class
did it and made sure we noticed.
Saw envy in our faces
yet knew we'd never tell.

## **Duet**

Her share flat to themselves
        close on the couch

Ella and Louis on the record player
        gas heater sputtering

their double bowing hearts
        pulsing with the love songs

his thrilling mouth   her fervent response
        their searching fingers

consummation of their frustrated desire
        without going all the way.

## Ukulele boys

First year teaching at a country school
she has some hard-case kids

whose families sing each Friday night
and drink their wages.

Some of the boys bring in their ukuleles.
She learns to strum old folk songs

like 'The Fox' and 'Oh Susannah'.
Singing becomes the high point of the day

but during reading, writing, sums
attentions wander   personalities (not hers) take over.

Big Brook, black fuzz on upper lip, is class bad boy.
His defiance holds her captive.

Drained by defeat she co-opts a male teacher
to punish him but is punished in her turn.

His hard, accusing eyes.
Her guilt.

Yet others   Honi, Tim, Tipene
still dance brown fingers over ukulele strings

their easy going natures rocking the classroom
into a state of truce.

# Right of passage

Music can change the world
– Ludwig van Beethoven

## Sibelius 2

At a church dance
refuge for souls
searching for a mate
they find each other

he agnostic
she lonely.

An energetic dancer
he makes her laugh.
Their politics align.

First date is in the Botanic Gardens
lush with rainforest
tuis' bells
hothouse begonias.

While they picnic near the pond
she hears the story of his life
and his dreams of brilliancy in academe.

His vision excites her
and later, sprawled on the floor
in his small student flat
they listen to Sibelius

the symphony sustaining
the promise of the day
with grandiose motifs
and hints of *sturm und drang*.

Nineteen, in love
she resonates with the perfect pitch
of his fantastic future.

## Sibelius 2 reprised

On their first over-ocean flight
they hold each other's gold-ringed hands.

His professor, charming, urbane
meets them at the postage-stamp airport
and drives them to his home
a pine-ringed eyrie above the university
boats' lights on the black river below.

His wife serves dinner
and after food and academic conversation
he dims the lights and plays Sibelius 2.
It feels like an initiation rite.

The music once more
seizes her with its passion
but doubt mutes her.

Can they be happy in this place –
he a part of the scientific brotherhoods
she a quaver on an empty stave?

## Vaughan Williams' 5th Symphony

The Romanza movement tells me
what kept us linked
in those fraught times

confined to a small apartment
with its other-worldly view
where conflict became our dark habit

often I ran from you
nerves screaming to be released
from the underside of wedded bliss

you took the vinyl record from its sleeve
compelling us to sit and listen
to the gently swelling harmonies

letting Vaughan Williams sing us back
until our souls returned.

## Some moments

Cherishing me
our unborn child
in quiet moments
upon waking
and before sleep

shared rapture
in a song
a symphony
a perfect riff
that moment when
notes   phrases
expand   resolve
make sense of life

the joyful running
of our children to your
outstretched arms
(one arm for each)
to claim your full attention
when they could

hearing the dawn bird chorus
understanding now
how it reverberated
in a part of you
kept secret   sacrosanct
well hidden
in a place
I'd never reach.

# Right of passage

As families flock to wonder at
Pettit and Sevitt project homes
in an architecture documentary
nostalgia spools me to the sixties
its vision   aspirations   experiment

the clinker bricks   bronzed timber
clean white walls of dwellings
designed to disappear into their setting
like tawny frogmouths in a stringybark
not seek to dominate
as brash buildings of this century may do

ah!   the temper of those times!
a middle-class young family's dream
not merely mortar   bricks
but ART
a block of wild-flowered land our piece of paradise
no lifetime-dragging burden but our right of passage.

# Jerusalem

In time of an approaching war
(when were they ever not expecting war)

a steel-clad bus takes us from Tel Aviv
along the midnight road to Jerusalem.

Our children, with cherubs' faces, sleep.
Beyond, there's blackness as menacing

as soldiers cradling machine guns.
Outside the Jaffa Gate, a sudden samaritan

sees us, fearful, stranded with our luggage
drives us from gate to gate

until he finds our lodgings: sparse, safe,
the Jewish landlord surprisingly

sanguine about our 3 a.m. arrival.
At dawn, the muezzin's piercing call

jolts us into the reality of this walled world,
pale rock first hammered 6,000 years ago

now bleached clean of millennia of blood.
Arab taxi drivers nurse radios for news of war,

babel of languages mingle in the Shuk,
buy, sell kosher and halal meats

baklava, pomegranates, spices, wine.
Black-garbed priests and rabbis stroll cobbled streets.

Outside tiny cafés men smoke, drink Turkish coffee.
Our children make friends with Arab children in a park.

We're dazzled by the blue-gold of the Dome,
witness heaven in the Holy Sepulchre,

trace the Stations of the Cross.
In the Abbell Synagogue, light streams

from Chagall's stained-glass windows,
haloing us in hope.

# Calcutta

Around a small stage in a grand hotel
redolent of incense, cardamon and English breakfasts

where *shudra* spend their nights sleeping
on the floor outside guest room doors,

an audience reclines, bowls of daze-inducing
*mithai* at their fingertips

entranced by a dancer's swirling red silk skirt,
bangles on her wrists and ankles singing

to the beat of *tabla* players, cross-legged,
talking with their hands.

On a footpath very close to the hotel
under a beach umbrella and a blue tarpaulin,

a mother stirs fish curry on a tiny brazier.
Oblivious of street vendors' raucous calls,

men washing at a pavement well,
and a Brahmin cow staring down the traffic,

a young boy bends his head, straining to read
by torchlight, finger tracing words.

A father drills his son in English: the only chance,
he says, for Dev to have a better life

# Journey from the centre of the earth

There's a stirring in her withered wings.
With his urging, she joins the choir that will
    celebrate the opening of the mineral exhibition.

Fusion of rock and classical music fires her
its red hot lava feeds a remnant self
    she'd thought was dead.

The explorers' subterranean struggles mirror hers
their pleas of *save me save me* echo her own
    the women's chorale sings her home.

Surviving the horror of the monsters' boneyard
– their crocodile teeth and bloodshot eyes –
    she rides the choral chariot into the buried cathedral

where chandeliers blaze crystal quartz.
As the cantata reaches its zenith
    she erupts from the centre of the earth

in synchrony with the synthesiser's
saw-toothed pulse.
    Her body   psychedelic   blinds him.

# That houri's dance

Eyes I dare not meet in dreams – T.S. Eliot

T.S. thought he knew a thing
or two about the Shadow
implied disquietment
beneath each joy

hinted at our penchant
for complacency
warned us to be
suspicious, alert, aware.

We all know something
of that houri's dance
that it can writhe and sway
in demi-monde of our desires

know it can enthral, beguile
allure and beckon
into an endless dark –
our private bedlam.

# The hardest word

those times when he put on his headphones
sang that song  over  and  over  off-key  until
her shattered nerves hung like entrails on the CD player
and she wished Elton John had never been born
when he shuttered himself away from questions
scratched on soundproof walls
as she and their children clawed to break through
the sarcophagus of his isolation
she still thought he was singing it to her.

# Resurrection

Singing the 'Hallelujah Chorus'
at one with the voices of a hundred

she's alive, the last of her bonds broken.
The trumpet sounds for her –

banish the shadow!
be real once more!

Singing 'Worthy is the Lamb'
swings her up to glory clouds

her independent self proclaimed.
As the 'Amen Chorus'

uplifts the audience
she's aware of someone

in the front row
face upturned

feels the heat of his enraptured gaze –
trusts he'll lead her, not astray

but into a future of tranquillity.

## Listening to Tchaikovsky

Tchaikovsky's Symphony
– the Fifth

is playing on FM radio
and she's back in the tiny hillside flat

they'd played it when Gordon
came to dinner with his girlfriend

there was mutual appraisal
and clever conversation

did Gordon bring the record?
the three of them (not Belinda) were aficionados

Gordon with long fair hair
slight body   club foot

a fellow surplus teacher
she could laugh with

in the uncertainty of new marriage
in a new country

as the final movement strides
towards its climax

she sits in her psychologist's waiting room
listening to Tchaikovsky.

# Cameo

You are the music while the music lasts
– T.S. Eliot

# Cameo at Hanging Rock

Three young girls dressed in white
heartbeats pulsing with cicadas
Botticelli hair floating

sleepwalk in eucalyptus-perfumed air
through summer-scorched grass
as golden as a Streeton landscape

allured by panpipes' haunting purity
to explore rock formations
redolent of Ancients' sacred presence

a cameo edged with a piano's molten teardrops
etched deeply into my memory
a photogravure of exquisite foreboding.

## Womadelaide 2001

In the forty-degree heat of Botanic Park
flags hang like wet washing.

Jimmie Little, in an orange jacket
sings to the adoring crowd
but halfway through the song
trips   falls
the audience shocked into silence
then cheering as he is up
with smiling comment
to sing again.

Close to the stage
a young girl shyly dances
and a child walks slowly across the grass
on thin black legs
wearing an army cap
Hawaiian shirt and shorts
pink bag slung across her body
chatting on a mobile phone.

# Libertango

One winter's evening
in an old asylum's grounds
there's a hub of warmth –
coffee, conversation, music

where a diminutive young woman
dances her bow across her double bass
syncopating with guitar
playing the 'Libertango'.

They have the audience –
folk followers, musicians
poets, singers
maybe even shades of troubled souls

clapping, tapping their feet
swaying, smiling
surrendering their bodies to the seductive beat
of a sultry Buenos Aires night.

## Philip Glass in Florence

In the Piazza della Signoria
green-lit David
a breathless crowd and I
wait for Philip Glass.

First night alone in Florence
I've come upon
an outdoor concert
by the master of minimalism.

I wedge myself against
a trattoria fence
entwined with ivy
between Americans and Swedes

leaves brushing my face
cobbles cold beneath me
the sky hot midnight blue.
Folding his lanky frame

onto the piano stool
head bent
Glass begins to play
his layered, hypnotic compositions

his fingers entrancing us
into a fourth dimension
until it's over and we erupt
with frenzied applause.

Afterwards
sipping lemonade
I join promenaders
who stroll with families and dogs

and on the Ponte Vecchio
jewelled shop windows
glow with luminosity
to rival Florence sun.

# Mahler 1

His genius still draws bows
across my body as I sit with seagulls
in winter sunlight.

He was despised for his first symphony
its sweeping musicality
its daring, glorious, sardonic cadences
of death, life, love.

Shocked patrons dropped their fans
paled at the audacity of harmony
the letting out   the letting go.

Today hope is reborn from love's rejection.
Gelmetti clasps his hands, head bowed
pounds   three   last   chords
then relinquishes control for Mahler's sake.

The culmination brings us to our feet
then out into the world
to face our imitations of reality.

# Pavane

Music heals us. It says 'you are not alone'
– Anna Goldsworthy

## Pavane

Above the Binney hills
the seabirds' flight

cascading rain streaks
columns grey and white

the gull that gulped
our bread has flown

and parents drag
reluctant children home

thinking sunshine here
has had its day

though still it shines
on our side of the bay

where we in silence
satisfied, replete

watch waves in slow pavane
advance, retreat…

## Leonard Cohen was a brave man

(for Ted)

Showed yourself to me half-opened
lives laid bare though not completely

wisdom sweated from a fire box
novice turn about with teacher

glowing gifts for me to carry
packages of hard-learnt lessons

dreamed that night a day together
friendship, closeness, joy of living

whither from this place of beauty
muted roar of waves on shoreline

tui calls in remnant forest
whither with my solitude?

# Water music

You once told me that when a boy
your first paid job was tending rowing boats
on the River Ouse.

I see you – eager, nervous
meticulous in carrying out your tasks:
cleaning, rowing, mooring.

You rowed us on the lake in Pukekura Park
and again in ancient Knaresborough
where a viaduct bestrides the River Nidd.

The to and fro of your arms made water music.
I was mesmerised by the rhythm
your far-away gaze, the shape of your mouth.

Afterwards we drank coffee at the river-side tearoom
as the warmth of the day haloed us with love
and the river mirrored our happiness.

## Every time we say goodbye…

One morning, over sea miles
        you sang for me
we knew the song
        knew major became minor
emotions see-sawing
        from threnody to jubilate
lives as different in their scoring
        as Palestrina from Prokofiev
re-capitulated separations
        playing us shrill
reunions – impossibly –
        an epithalamium.

# Loch Lomond

Nicola Benedetti's on Classic FM
        her joyous violin playing
songs of her homeland
        that take me back to Scotland.

While we drove you sang every Scottish song
        you ever knew
brave baritone enhanced
        by the soft brogue you did so well.

The afternoon we came upon the loch
        your monsters lay quiescent
as you scanned the waters –
        wide open to the metaphysical

to the occult
        to ancient magic
hoping Nessie
        would reveal herself that day.

## Jupiter again

Today I listen to Holst's 'Jupiter' with joy.
I've come to love your funeral processional

>	the quasi-anthem
>	its triumphal march.

Today it thrills me and uplifts me
and I know that you are waiting

deep within the greatest anthem
at one with the vast silence of the cosmos.

## Leura Gardens

while travelling by train
to this place we visited so often

a reservoir of tears presses against my ribs

i do not want this pain to fill
the hollow of your absence

images of our time together
explode behind my eyes

*The Lark Ascending* plays to my inner ear

cherry trees in blossom line the streets
like flower girls at a wedding

the gardens flaunt their colours
i wear the striped jumper we bought here

and at the Waldorf Gardens Resort
a jazz group plays 'Mood Indigo'

under the spent wisteria

## Little Golden Bay

On this small
stony beach
h-rurrrush   h-rurrrush
of waves
evokes a childhood
East Coast expedition

my parents
and a caravan
of floating each night
into sea dreams
waking
to sea music

the sound brings
extraordinary ease
an almost happiness
a knowing
that all's in its place
as perfect now
as it will ever be.

# Notes

Opus or the shortened form Op. after the title of a piece of music means 'work'.

p. 11. VJ Day: Victory over Japan Day, 15 August 1945 on which Imperial Japan surrendered, in effect bringing World War II to an end

p. 14. Festival of Nine Lessons and Carols, traditional Church of England Christmas celebration

p. 16. *A Young Person's Guide to the Orchestra*, Benjamin Britten

p. 17. Cornel Wilde, lead actor in the film *A Song to Remember*
Polonaise Op. 53 in A Flat major, Frédéric Chopin

p. 18. Piano Concerto No 2, Sergei Rachmaninov

p. 19. *The Student Prince*, film with dubbed singing by tenor Mario Lanza
*Gaudeamus Igitur*, an academic song mainly performed at university graduation ceremonies

p. 20. 'Moon River', theme for film *Breakfast at Tiffany's*

p. 21. Concerto for Two Violins in D minor, J.S. Bach
*The Go-Between*, by L.P. Hartley. Kahlil Gibran drawings
Andante: walking pace
Adagio: slow and stately

p. 34. Air on a G String, second movement of Johann Sebastian Bach's Orchestral Suite No. 3 in D major

p. 37. 'Rock Around the Clock' – Bill Haley and his Comets

p. 38. 'Softly Awakes My Heart', *Samson and Delilah*, opera by Camille Saint Saens

p. 39. Symphony No. 2, Johannes Brahms
New Zealand poets: Charles Brasch, James K Baxter, J. C. Beaglehole, Allen Curnow, Alistair Campbell, A.R.D. Fairburn, Louis Johnson, R.A.K. Mason and Anton Voght.

p. 42. *The Dream of Gerontius* (oratorio), *Enigma Variations*, Pomp and Circumstance March No. 1 ('Land of Hope and Glory') and Cello Concerto in E minor, Op. 85, played by Jacqueline du Pré; all composed by Edward Elgar

p. 45. Dave Brubeck Quartet, American jazz group

p. 46. Concerto for Two Harpsichords in C minor, Johann Sebastian Bach

p. 48. *The Ultimate Duets*, Ella Fitzgerald & Louis Armstrong

p. 53. Symphony No. 2, Jan Sibelius

p. 58. Pettit and Sevitt, Sydney project home designer

p. 59. The Islamic Call to Prayer
p. 60. Marc Chagall, artist
p. 61. Calcutta: Kolkata
*shudra:* servant class
*mithai:* sweetmeats, desserts
*tabla*: hand drums
p. 62. *Journey to the Centre of the Earth*, rock cantata, Rick Wakeman
p. 64. 'Sorry seems to be the hardest word', song by Elton John and Bernie Taupin
p. 65. *Messiah*, oratorio, George Frideric Handel
p. 66. Symphony No. 5, Pyotr Ilyich Tchaikovsky
p. 69. Panpipes by Gheorghe Zamfir
Piano Concerto No. 5 in E flat major, Beethoven, the slow movement, sound track for the film *Picnic at Hanging Rock*
p. 70. World Music Festival, Adelaide
p. 71. 'Libertango', Astor Piazzolla
p. 72. Philip Glass, minimalist composer and pianist
p. 74. Symphony No. 1 in D major, Gustav Mahler conducted by Gianluigi Gelmetti
p. 77. Pavane: dance popular in the 16th and 17th centuries
Don Binney, artist
p. 78. Leonard Cohen, poet, singer and songwriter
p. 80. 'Every Time We Say Goodbye', song by Cole Porter
p. 81. Nicola Benedetti, violinist
p. 82. *The Planets*, Gustav Holst
Last stanza is paraphrased from Ted Rutter's poem 'Walk the Walk'
p. 83. *The Lark Ascending*, Ralph Vaughan Williams

www.ingramcontent.com/pod-product-compliance
Lightning Source LLC
Chambersburg PA
CBHW071025080526
44587CB00015B/2505